Implementing the Common Core State Standards

with *Pearson Algebra 1, Geometry, Algebra 2*

Boston, Massachusetts • Chandler, Arizona • Glenview, Illinois • Upper Saddle River, New Jersey

ISBN-13: 978-0-13-318558-4
ISBN-10: 0-13-318558-3
5 6 7 8 9 10 V011 16 15 14 13 12

Contents

About *This Guide*

Pearson is pleased to offer this Guide to Implementing the Common Core State Standards as a complement to its *Pearson High School Mathematics Common Core Edition*. In this Guide, you will find information about the Common Core State Standards that can be useful as you look to implement a curriculum based on the Common Core State Standards.

On pages 4 through 6, you will find two monographs written by Pearson authors Randall Charles and Grant Wiggins. In **Focus and Coherence,** Dr. Charles make explicit the connection between the organization of the Common Core State Standards and *Pearson High School Mathematics Common Core Edition*. In **Fostering Understanding,** Dr. Wiggins discusses the emphasis on understanding that is key to the Common Core State Standards and germane to *Pearson High School Mathematics Common Core Edition*.

You'll find an overview of the Common Core State Standards for Mathematics on pages 7 through 27, with first a discussion of the **Standards for Mathematical Practice** in *Pearson High School Mathematics Common Core Edition* on pages 7 through 21, followed by a look at the **Standards for Mathematical Content** for High School (pages 22–27).

Next we present information about the upcoming common assessments being developed by the two consortia, the **Partnership for Assessment of Readiness for College and Careers** and **SMARTER Balanced Assessment Consortium** (pages 28–30).

On pages 31 and 32 is an **Observational Protocol** that you can use to monitor your students' progress towards developing proficiency with the Standards for Mathematical Practice. You can reproduce this protocol from this guide or you can download the protocol from PowerAlgebra.com or PowerGeometry.com in the Teacher Resources.

We've included a **Parent Letter** that offers some information about the Common Core State Standards for parents as well as a **Parent's Guide to the Standards for Mathematical Practice.** The Parent's Guide suggests questions that parents can ask their sons or daughters as they work on homework exercises. Both of these are also available as a download from PowerAlgebra.com or PowerGeometry.com in the Teacher Resources.

Pages 35 through 51 show **Correlations of all of the Standards for Mathematical Content for High School** and indicate where the standards are addressed throughout *Pearson High School Mathematics Common Core Edition (Algebra 1, Geometry,* and *Algebra 2)*. You'll notice that although most of the (+) standards are expected to be taught in a fourth-year mathematics course, many of them are covered in Pearson's three-year course sequence.

Common Core State Standards
for Mathematics

The Common Core State Standards Initiative is a state-led initiative coordinated by the National Governors Association Center for Best Practices (NGA Center) and the Council of Chief State School Officers (CCSSO), with a goal of developing a set of standards in mathematics and in English language arts that would be implemented in many, if not most states in the United States.

> These standards identify the knowledge and skills students should gain throughout their K-12 careers so that upon graduation from high school. they will be college- or career-ready.

The Common Core State Standards for Mathematics (CCSSM) were developed by mathematicians and math educators and reviewed by many professional groups and state department of education representatives of the 48 participating states. The members of the writing committee looked at state standards from high-performing states in the United States and from high-performing countries around the world and developed standards that reflect the intent and content of these exemplars.

The final draft was released in June 2010 after nearly 12 months of intense development, review, and revision. To date, over 40 states have adopted these new standards and are currently working to develop model curricula or curriculum frameworks based on these standards.

These standards identify the knowledge and skills students should gain throughout their K–12 careers so that upon graduation from high school. they will be college- or career-ready. The standards include rigorous content and application of knowledge through higher-order thinking skills.

The CCSSM consist of two interrelated sets of standards, the Standards for Mathematical Practice and the Standards for Mathematical Content. **The Standards for Mathematical Practice** describe the processes, practices, and dispositions that lead to mathematical proficiency. The eight standards are common to all grade levels, K–12, highlighting that these processes, practices, and dispositions are developed throughout one's school career. A discussion of these standards is found on pages 7 to 21.

The **Standards for Mathematical Content** are grade-specific for Kindergarten through Grade 8; at the high school level, the standards are not structured by course or grade; rather they are organized into six conceptual categories. Within each conceptual category are domains and clusters, which each consists of one or more standards. Most of the standards are meant to be covered by the end of Algebra 2; a few standards, indicated with (+), are generally addressed in advanced high school mathematics courses. An overview of these standards for high School is found on pages 22 to 27.

Focus and Coherence
Monograph by Randall I. Charles

> What and how students are taught should reflect not only the topics that fall within a certain academic discipline, but also the key ideas that determine how knowledge is organized and generated within that discipline.*

The Common Core State Standards for Mathematics (CCSSM), released in June 2010, represent the work of numerous mathematicians and mathematics educators concerned about the state of K–12 mathematics education in the United States. A primary goal of the developers of the CCSSM was to respond to the criticism of mathematics curricula in the United States being a mile wide and an inch deep by providing a roadmap to "more **focused and coherent** [curricula] in order to improve mathematics achievement in this country" (CCSSM 2010, 3). *Pearson High School Mathematics Common Core Edition* fully embraces the focus and coherence called for in the CCSSM, and expands upon them in a significant way.

A focused and coherent mathematics curriculum provides in-depth instruction on a limited number of important categories of mathematics content. CCSSM identifies and organizes these important categories of mathematics content standards, to which *Pearson High School Mathematics Common Core Edition* is directly aligned, and calls them conceptual categories: **Number and Quantity, Algebra, Functions, Modeling, Geometry** and **Statistics and Probability.** Each of the six **conceptual categories** further organizes related content into **domains** and each domain organizes related content standards into **clusters.** Every chapter in *Pearson High School Mathematics Common Core Edition* correlates to the CCSSM conceptual categories, domains, and content clusters.

Pearson High School Mathematics Common Core Edition is unique in that it extends focus and coherence beyond just providing in-depth instruction on a limited

FIGURE 1

Conceptual Category	Big Ideas in Pearson's High School Mathematics
Number & Quantity	• Properties • Equivalence • Proportionality
Algebra	• Properties • Variable • Equivalence • Proportionality • Solving Equations and Inequalities
Functions	• Variable • Function • Equivalence
Modeling	• Modeling • Function
Geometry	• Visualization • Transformations • Measurement • Reasoning & Proof • Similarity • Coordinate Geometry
Statistics & Probability	• Data Collection & Analysis • Data Representation • Probability

number of important categories of mathematics content. The program extends focus and coherence by making explicit the Big Ideas in mathematics that students need to know and by showing how those ideas are related. A Big Idea in mathematics —called a Key Idea in the CCSSM— is a statement of an idea that is central to learning mathematics; it links numerous smaller ideas—called Essential Understandings in *Pearson High School Mathematics Common Core Edition* into a coherent whole (Charles 2005). *Pearson High School Mathematics Common Core Edition* connects all CCSSM content standards to Big Ideas. Figure 1 shows how the Big Ideas from *Pearson High School Mathematics Common Core Edition* align with the conceptual categories of the CCSSM.

Notice that several Big Ideas run across conceptual categories; they connect ideas across content topics, and this is one reason they are "big." To illustrate this, Figure 2 shows the Big Idea called Equivalence and gives examples of content topics in different conceptual categories.

These Big Ideas are listed in student-accessible language in the front of each Student Edition. Including this listing is important, but it does not always convey to students their power. To do this, Big Ideas are translated into student-friendly Essential Questions presented at the beginning of each chapter (see Figure 3). **Essential Questions** focus students' attention on what they will be learning throughout a chapter and what they will be able to do and understand at the end of a chapter. Essential Questions are revisited at the end of each chapter where answers are given.

Conclusion – Why do focus and coherence matter?

A focused and coherent mathematics curriculum makes possible in-depth student understanding, which in turn leads to higher student achievement. Knowing that the myriad of content topics in the high school mathematics curriculum coalesce into six conceptual categories helps students understand mathematics – they see the "whole," not just the "parts." And, when students know that mathematics is grounded on Big Ideas not just skills, and that those ideas are connected, they better understand mathematics. *Pearson High School Mathematics Common Core Edition* embraces and enhances the focus and coherence vision of the CCSSM leading to higher achievement and college and career readiness for all.

FIGURE 2

Conceptual Categories	Big Idea
Number & Quantity …explain why the rectangular and polar forms of a given complex number represent the same number. (N.CN.4)	**Equivalence** • A single quantity may be represented by many different expressions. • The facts about a quantity may be expressed by many different equations (or inequalities).
Algebra Choose and produce an equivalent form of an expression…(A.SSE.3)	
Functions Write a function defined by an expression in different but equivalent forms to reveal and explain different properties of the function. (F.IF.8)	

FIGURE 3

Chapter: Exponents and Exponential Functions

Big Idea	Essential Questions
Equivalence	How can you represent very large and very small numbers?
Properties	How can you simplify expressions involving exponents?
Function	What are the essential characteristics of exponential functions?

References

Charles, Randall I. "Big Ideas and Understandings as The Foundation for Elementary and Middle School Mathematics," *Journal of Matheamtics Education Leadership 8, no. 1* (2005): 9–24.

*Common Core State Standards Initiative. Common Core State Standards for Mathematics. Washington, D.C., (2010).

Fostering Understanding
Monograph by Grant Wiggins

It should seem obvious that the point of instruction in mathematics is **understanding** as reflected in effective problem-solving. Alas, too often mathematics instruction is focused on topic coverage and "plug and chug" work rather than on genuine student connections and transfer of learning. Students too often spend valuable instructional time completing computational exercises with a goal of procedural fluency and sparse attention on developing deeper conceptual understanding or strategic competence that would help them become effective and efficient problem-solvers.

> ## Those content standards are potential "points of intersection" between the Standards for Mathematical Content and the Standards for Mathematical Practice.

The recently released Common Core State Standards for Mathematics (CCSSM) have articulated the goal of **deep mathematical understanding.** This goal is made clear in at least two ways: the focus on understanding is stressed in the introduction; and curriculum, instruction and assessment are expected to mesh the Standards for Mathematical Practice with the Standards for Mathematical Content. "Those content standards which set an expectation of understanding are potential 'points of intersection' between the Standards for Mathematical Content and the Standards for Mathematical Practice" (CCSSM 2010, 8).

Understanding by Design is built on this same purpose of developing and deepening student understanding, and thus can provide a useful strategy and set of tools for honoring the spirit and letter of the Common Core State Standards for Mathematics. What's the key? The authors of the CCSSM astutely clarify the aim by focusing on the **assessment** implications (just as we demand in Understanding by Design):

> Asking a student to understand something means asking a teacher to assess whether the student has understood it...One hallmark of mathematical understanding is the ability to justify, in a way appropriate to the student's mathematical maturity, why a particular mathematical statement is true or where a mathematical rule comes from. (CCSSM 2010, 4)

Know-how is necessary but insufficient. Real understanding and problem-solving requires knowing why. Only then can learners adapt prior learning—transfer their learning—to future problems. Students who really understand can apply their learning flexibly and creatively; they are able to use content, not just recall math facts.

Pearson High School Mathematics Common Core Edition focuses on helping students develop **deep conceptual understanding** of the mathematics they encounter and **strong problem-solving and reasoning abilities,** with the goal of ensuring that students understand and are able to do mathematics.

Look closer at the second half of the key phrase—**understand and be able to do**—to see that the authors are stressing the goal of transfer, not mere recall of discrete skill on typical quizzes. The focus is on deep conceptual understanding and strategic competence of that understanding. The CCSSM call for **a new approach to thinking about and teaching mathematics.** *Pearson High School Mathematics Common Core Editions* offer a program grounded in conceptual understanding and reasoning to help students become mathematically proficient.

References
Common Core State Standards Initiative. *Common Core State Standards for Mathematics.* Washington, D.C., 2010.

Standards for
Mathematical Practice

The Standards for Mathematical Practice are an important part of the Common Core State Standards. They describe varieties of proficiency that teachers should focus on helping their students develop. These practices draw from the NCTM Process Standards of problem solving, reasoning and proof, communication, representation, and connections and the strands of mathematical proficiency specified in the National Research Council's report *Adding It Up*: adaptive reasoning, strategic competence, conceptual understanding, procedural fluency, and productive disposition.

We present an overview of the features of *Pearson High School Mathematics Common Core Edition* that help students develop proficiency in each of the Standards for Mathematical Practice.

1 Make sense of problems and persevere in solving them.

2 Reason abstractly and quantitatively.

3 Construct viable arguments and critique the reasoning of others.

4 Model with mathematics.

5 Use appropriate tools strategically.

6 Attend to precision.

7 Look for and make use of structure.

8 Look for and express regularity in repeated reasoning.

1 MAKE SENSE OF PROBLEMS AND PERSEVERE IN SOLVING THEM.

Mathematically proficient students start by explaining to themselves the meaning of a problem and looking for entry points to its solution. They analyze givens, constraints, relationships, and goals. They make conjectures about the form and meaning of the solution and plan a solution pathway rather than simply jumping into a solution attempt. They consider analogous problems, and try special cases and simpler forms of the original problem in order to gain insight into its solution. They monitor and evaluate their progress and change course if necessary. Older students might, depending on the context of the problem, transform algebraic expressions or change the viewing window on their graphing calculator to get the information they need. Mathematically proficient students can explain correspondences between equations, verbal descriptions, tables, and graphs wor draw diagrams of important features and relationships, graph data, and search for regularity or trends. Younger students might rely on using concrete objects or pictures to help conceptualize and solve a problem. Mathematically proficient students check their answers to problems using a different method, and they continually ask themselves, "Does this make sense?" They can understand the approaches of others to solving complex problems and identify correspondences between different approaches.

The **Solve It!**, the opener for each lesson, presents a problem situation for which students work collaboratively or individually. The Solve It! offers opportunities for students to **make sense of problems** and persevere in solving them. Guiding questions in the Teacher's Editions help students **persevere to find entries into the problems** and to **develop a workable solution plan.**

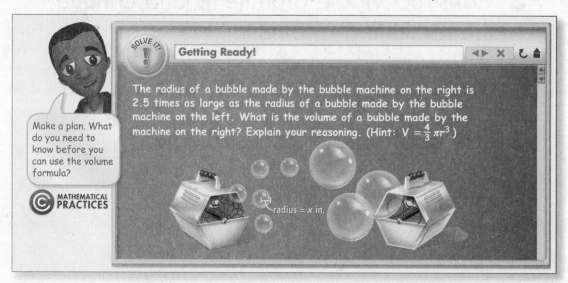

Students look to **understand the meaning** of the problem presented and **develop and implement a solution plan.** The rich visual support helps students make sense of problem situations.

The **Know-Need-Plan** boxes help students **analyze the givens** in the problem and **develop a workable solution plan.**

Know	Need	Plan
• The function for the acorn's height • The initial height is 20 ft.	The function's graph and the time the acorn hits the ground	Use a table of values to graph the function. Use the graph to estimate when the acorn hits the ground.

The **Think, Plan** boxes model through questions and answers the thinking that proficient problem solvers use.

Think

Have you seen a problem like this one?
Yes. Finding percent increase is like finding percent decrease. The difference is in calculating the amount of increase or decrease.

Think

How are the speeds related?
The air speed is a plane's speed with no wind. Add wind speed and air speed to get the ground speed with a tailwind. Subtract wind speed from air speed to find the ground speed with a headwind.

Some remind students to **look for similar or analogous problem situations** that they previously solved. Others focus on understanding the relationships among the variables or quantities in the problem.

Throughout the exercise sets, students are called on to make sense of the problems they encounter and find workable solution plans to solve them. With the **Think About a Plan** exercises, students **understand the meaning** of the problem situation, **analyze the givens** in a problem situation, and **develop a solution plan.**

 59. Think About a Plan Suppose a family wants to buy the house advertised at the right. They have $60,000 for a down payment. Their mortgage will have an annual interest rate of 6%. The loan is to be repaid over a 30-yr period. How much will it cost the family to repay this mortgage over the 30 yr?
  • What information can you obtain from the formula above?
  • How can you use the information given by the formula to solve the problem?

As you work through the lessons, consider asking these questions to help your students develop proficiency with this standard:

• What is the problem that you are solving for?
• What problem have you recently solved that might be similar to this one?
• How will you go about solving the problem? (that is, What's your plan?)
• Are you progressing towards a solution? How do you know? Should you try a different solution plan?
• Did you check your solution by using a different method?

2 REASON ABSTRACTLY AND QUANTITATIVELY.

Mathematically proficient students make sense of quantities and their relationships in problem situations. They bring two complementary abilities to bear on problems involving quantitative relationships: the ability to decontextualize—to abstract a given situation and represent it symbolically and manipulate the representing symbols as if they have a life of their own, without necessarily attending to their referents—and the ability to contextualize, to pause as needed during the manipulation process in order to probe into the referents for the symbols involved. Quantitative reasoning entails habits of creating a coherent representation of the problem at hand; considering the units involved; attending to the meaning of quantities, not just how to compute them; and knowing and flexibly using different properties of operations and objects.

Reasoning is one of the guiding principles of *Pearson High School Mathematics Common Core Edition*. The **Think, Plan** boxes guide students to **represent problem situations symbolically.** Some offer prompts to help students represent a situation symbolically and to **manipulate the symbols** in an equation.

Think

Why does $y = x - 2$ represent the boundary line?
For any value of x, the corresponding value of y is the boundary between values of y that are greater than $x - 2$ and values of y that are less than $x - 2$.

Think

Why do you substitute 0 for y to find the x-intercept?
The x-intercept is the x-coordinate of a point on the x-axis. Any point on the x-axis has a y-coordinate of 0.

Others remind students to **identify the referents of solutions.**

Think

What does the solution represent in the real world?
Check what the assigned variables represent. Here, (20, 40) represents 20 large snack packs and 40 small snack packs.

Think

Does it make sense that two different prices can yield the same profit?
Yes. You can generate a given profit either by selling many CDs at a low price, or fewer CDs at a high price.

As you work through the lessons, consider asking these questions to help your students develop proficiency with this standard:

- Can you write or recall an expression or equation to match the problem situation?
- What do the numbers or variables in the equation refer to?
- What's the connection among the numbers and variables in the equation?

Do you UNDERSTAND?  **MATHEMATICAL PRACTICES**

6. Vocabulary How is the property for raising a quotient to a power similar to the property for raising a product to a power?

7. a. Reasoning Ross simplifies $\frac{a^3}{a^7}$ as shown at the right. Explain why Ross's method works.

$$\frac{a^3}{a^7} = \frac{1}{a^{7-3}} = \frac{1}{a^4}$$

b. Open-Ended Write a quotient of powers and use Ross's method to simplify it.

In the **Do You Understand?** feature, found at the end of each lesson, students **explain their thinking** related to the concepts studied in the lesson.

5. Reasoning How does each of the numbers a, b, and c affect the graph of a quadratic function $y = ax^2 + bx + c$?

The **Reasoning** exercises focus students' attention on the **structure or meaning of an operation** rather than the solution.

In the **Put It All Together,** students draw on their reasoning skills to put forth appropriate **symbolic representations of problems** presented.

Performance Task 3

Solve the problem. Show all of your work and explain your steps.

A town is organizing a Fourth of July parade. There will be two sizes of floats in the parade, as shown below. A space of 10 ft will be left after each float.

10-ft space | 30 ft | 10-ft space | 15 ft

a. Describe how the total length of the parade will be calculated.

b. The parade must be at least 150 ft long, but less than 200 ft long. What combinations of large and small floats are possible?

c. Large floats cost $600 to operate. Small floats cost $300 to operate. The town has a budget of $2500 to operate the floats. How does this change your answer to part (a)? What combinations of large and small floats are possible?

3 CONSTRUCT VIABLE ARGUMENTS AND CRITIQUE THE REASONING OF OTHERS.

Mathematically proficient students understand and use stated assumptions, definitions, and previously established results in constructing arguments. They make conjectures and build a logical progression of statements to explore the truth of their conjectures. They are able to analyze situations by breaking them into cases, and can recognize and use counterexamples. They justify their conclusions, communicate them to others, and respond to the arguments of others. They reason inductively about data, making plausible arguments that take into account the context from which the data arose. Mathematically proficient students are also able to compare the effectiveness of two plausible arguments, distinguish correct logic or reasoning from that which is flawed, and—if there is a flaw in an argument—explain what it is. Elementary students can construct arguments using concrete referents such as objects, drawings, diagrams, and actions. Such arguments can make sense and be correct, even though they are not generalized or made formal until later grades. Later, students learn to determine domains to which an argument applies. Students at all grades can listen or read the arguments of others, decide whether they make sense, and ask useful questions to clarify or improve the arguments.

Pearson High School Mathematics Common Core Edition has a strong focus on critical reasoning, argumentation, and critique of arguments. Students are often asked to explain their solutions and the thinking that led them to these solutions. The **Solve It!** activities always ask student to **justify their solutions and their reasoning.**

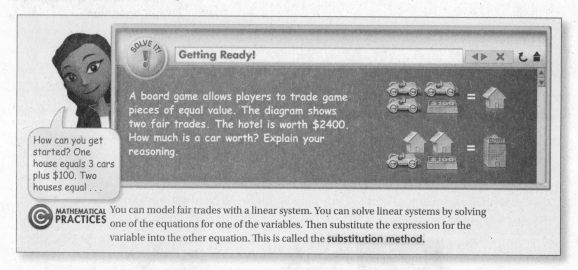

You can model fair trades with a linear system. You can solve linear systems by solving one of the equations for one of the variables. Then substitute the expression for the variable into the other equation. This is called the **substitution method.**

As you work through the lessons, consider asking these questions to help your students develop proficiency with this standard:

- What does your answer mean?
- How do you know that your answer is correct?
- If I told you I think the answer should be [a wrong answer], how would you explain to me why I'm wrong?

Many of the **Think-Plan** boxes focus on helping students **analyze situations, justify conclusions, and reason inductively and deductively.**

Plan

Can you solve this problem another way?

Yes. You could actually solve the equation to find any solutions. However, you only need to know the number of solutions, so use the discriminant.

Think

Does the location of the circumcenter make sense?

Yes, $\triangle POS$ is a right triangle, so its circumcenter should lie on its hypotenuse.

Throughout the program are exercises that ask students to construct arguments to defend their solutions and to respond to the solutions and arguments of others. In the **Reasoning** exercises, students are expected to **formulate arguments** to support their solutions.

 57. Reasoning The diagram at the right shows the dimensions of a kite. The length of the vertical blue crosspiece is s. What is the length of the horizontal red crosspiece in terms of s?

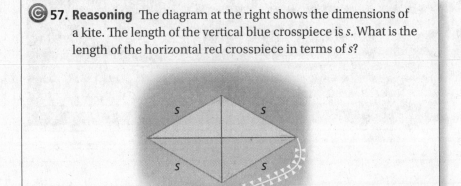

The **Error Analysis** exercises require students to **critique the solution** presented for a problem.

 42. Error Analysis A student graphed the function $y = \sqrt{x-2}$ at the right. What mistake did the student make? Draw the correct graph.

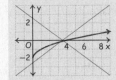

4 MODEL WITH MATHEMATICS.

Mathematically proficient students can apply the mathematics they know to solve problems arising in everyday life, society, and the workplace. In early grades, this might be as simple as writing an addition equation to describe a situation. In middle grades, a student might apply proportional reasoning to plan a school event or analyze a problem in the community. By high school, a student might use geometry to solve a design problem or use a function to describe how one quantity of interest depends on another. Mathematically proficient students who can apply what they know are comfortable making assumptions and approximations to simplify a complicated situation, realizing that these may need revision later. They are able to identify important quantities in a practical situation and map their relationships using such tools as diagrams, two-way tables, graphs, flowcharts and formulas. They can analyze those relationships mathematically to draw conclusions. They routinely interpret their mathematical results in the context of the situation and reflect on whether the results make sense, possibly improving the model if it has not served its purpose.

Throughout the program, students build mathematical models using visuals, such as graphs, tables, or drawings; equations, expressions, or functions; and tools, including technology. Students construct mathematical models for the real-life situations presented in the **Solve It!** activities.

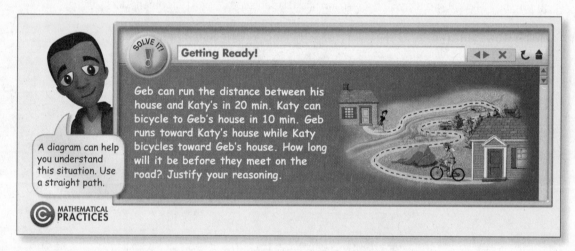

As you work through the lessons, consider asking these questions to help your students develop proficiency with this standard:

- What formula or relationship can you think of that fits this problem situation?
- What is the connection among the numbers in the problem?
- Is your answer reasonable? How do you know?
- What do the numbers in your solution refer to?

The visually rich problems facilitate understanding of the problem situations so students can connect to mathematical models more easily.

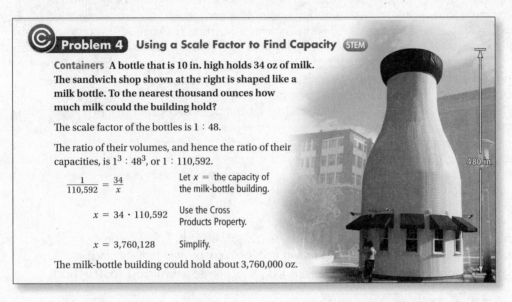

Problem 4 Using a Scale Factor to Find Capacity STEM

Containers A bottle that is 10 in. high holds 34 oz of milk. The sandwich shop shown at the right is shaped like a milk bottle. To the nearest thousand ounces how much milk could the building hold?

The scale factor of the bottles is 1 : 48.

The ratio of their volumes, and hence the ratio of their capacities, is $1^3 : 48^3$, or 1 : 110,592.

$$\frac{1}{110{,}592} = \frac{34}{x}$$ Let $x =$ the capacity of the milk-bottle building.

$x = 34 \cdot 110{,}592$ Use the Cross Products Property.

$x = 3{,}760{,}128$ Simplify.

The milk-bottle building could hold about 3,760,000 oz.

480 in.

In the **Pull It All Together** activities, student are often expected to **apply a mathematical model** to the situations presented.

BIG idea Modeling
You can model the trend of real-world data in a scatter plot with an equation of a line. You can use the equation to estimate or to make predictions.

©Performance Task 2

At the beginning of a 20-month period, Stacie owns one clothing store. During that period, she opens a second clothing store in a different location. The table shows the total monthly sales of Stacie's clothing stores for the 20-month period.

Monthly Sales (thousands of dollars)									
Month	2	4	6	8	10	12	14	16	18	20
Sales	3	5	4	6	5	12	16	22	26	32

a. When do you think the second store was opened? Justify your answer and include a graph in your justification.

5 USE APPROPRIATE TOOLS STRATEGICALLY.

Mathematically proficient students consider the available tools when solving a mathematical problem. These tools might include pencil and paper, concrete models, a ruler, a protractor, a calculator, a spreadsheet, a computer algebra system, a statistical package, or dynamic geometry software. Proficient students are sufficiently familiar with tools appropriate for their grade or course to make sound decisions about when each of these tools might be helpful, recognizing both the insight to be gained and their limitations. For example, mathematically proficient high school students analyze graphs of functions and solutions generated using a graphing calculator. They detect possible errors by strategically using estimation and other mathematical knowledge. When making mathematical models, they know that technology can enable them to visualize the results of varying assumptions, explore consequences, and compare predictions with data. Mathematically proficient students at various grade levels are able to identify relevant external mathematical resources, such as digital content located on a website, and use them to pose or solve problems. They are able to use technological tools to explore and deepen their understanding of concepts.

In *Pearson High School Mathematics Common Core Edition*, students become fluent in the use of a wide assortment of tools, ranging from physical devises to technology tools. Students are shown appropriate uses of various tools throughout the **Guided Instruction.**

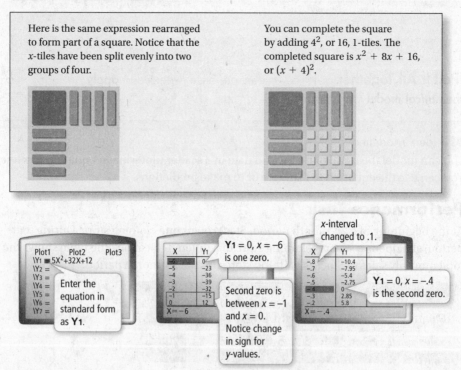

Here is the same expression rearranged to form part of a square. Notice that the x-tiles have been split evenly into two groups of four.

You can complete the square by adding 4^2, or 16, 1-tiles. The completed square is $x^2 + 8x + 16$, or $(x + 4)^2$.

Plot1 Plot2 Plot3
\Y1 = 5X²+32X+12
\Y2 =
\Y3 =
\Y4 = Enter the
\Y5 = equation in
\Y6 = standard form
\Y7 = as **Y1**.

Y1 = 0, $x = -6$ is one zero.

Second zero is between $x = -1$ and $x = 0$. Notice change in sign for y-values.

x-interval changed to .1.

Y1 = 0, $x = -.4$ is the second zero.

As you work through the lessons, consider asking these questions to help your students develop proficiency with this standard:

- What tools could you use to solve this problem? How can each one help you?
- Which tool is more useful for this problem? Explain your choice.
- Why is this tool better than [another tool mentioned]?
- Before you solve the problem, can you estimate the solution?

The **Activity Concept Bytes** often suggest tools to help students **develop fluency in the use of different tools.**

Activity

Find the product $(x + 4)(2x + 3)$.

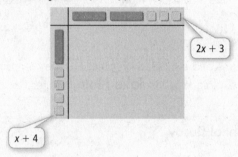

$2x + 3$

$x + 4$

The product is $2x^2 + 11x + 12$.

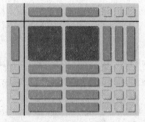

$2x^2 + 3x + 8x + 12$

$2x^2 + 11x + 12$ Add coefficients of like terms.

The **Technology Concept Bytes** focus on enhancing students' **strategic competence** with technology tools.

A graphing calculator can show the solutions of an inequality or a system of inequalities. To enter an inequality, press (apps) and scroll down to select **INEQUAL**. Move the cursor over the $=$ symbol for one of the equations. Notice the inequality symbols at the bottom of the screen, above the keys labeled **F2–F5**. Change the $=$ symbol to an inequality symbol by pressing (alpha) followed by one of **F2–F5**.

Activity 1

Graph the inequality $y < 3x - 7$.

1. Move the cursor over the $=$ symbol for Y_1. Press (alpha) and **F2** to select the $<$ symbol.

2. Enter the given inequality as Y_1.

3. Press (graph) to graph the inequality.

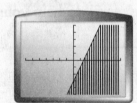

The **Choose a Method** exercises strengthens students' ability to articulate differences among tools, leading them to explain the **usefulness and appropriateness of different tools.**

 Choose a Method Choose paper and pencil, mental math, or a calculator to tell which measurement is greater.

31. 640 ft; 0.5 mi   **32.** 63 in.; 125 cm   **33.** 75 g; 5 oz

6 ATTEND TO PRECISION.

Mathematically proficient students try to communicate precisely to others. They try to use clear definitions in discussion with others and in their own reasoning. They state the meaning of the symbols they choose, including using the equal sign consistently and appropriately. They are careful about specifying units of measure, and labeling axes to clarify the correspondence with quantities in a problem. They calculate accurately and efficiently, express numerical answers with a degree of precision appropriate for the problem context. In the elementary grades, students give carefully formulated explanations to each other. By the time they reach high school they have learned to examine claims and make explicit use of definitions.

Students are expected to use mathematical terms and symbols with precision. Key terms are highlighted in each lesson and key concepts explained in the **Take Note** features.

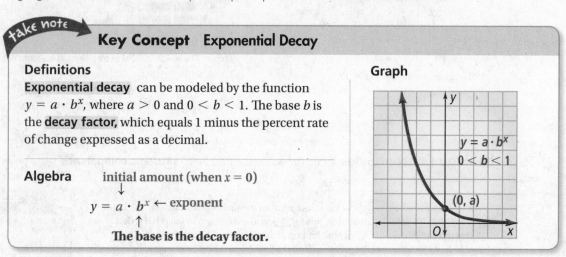

take note

Key Concept   Exponential Decay

Definitions
Exponential decay can be modeled by the function
$y = a \cdot b^x$, where $a > 0$ and $0 < b < 1$. The base b is the **decay factor,** which equals 1 minus the percent rate of change expressed as a decimal.

Algebra   initial amount (when $x = 0$)
                   ↓
        $y = a \cdot b^x$ ← exponent
                   ↑
        The base is the decay factor.

Graph

$y = a \cdot b^x$
$0 < b < 1$

$(0, a)$

As you work through the lessons, consider asking these questions to help your students develop proficiency with this standard:

- What do the symbols that you used mean?
- What units of measure are you using (for measurement problems)?
- What concepts or theorems did you use to solve the problem? How exactly do these relate to the problem?

Think

What are the units of the answer? You are cubing the radius, which is in meters (m), so your answer should be in cubic meters (m^3).

The **Think, Plan** boxes remind students to **use appropriate units of measure and accurate labels** when working through solutions.

In the **Do You UNDERSTAND?** feature, students revisit these key terms and **provide explicit definitions** or explanations of the terms.

> **Do you UNDERSTAND?**  **MATHEMATICAL PRACTICES**
>
> **7. Vocabulary** Identify the following in $\triangle RST$.
>   **a.** the hypotenuse
>   **b.** the segments of the hypotenuse
>   **c.** the segment of the hypotenuse adjacent to leg $\overline{ST}$
>
>

For the **Writing** exercises, students are expected to **provide clear, concise explanations** of terms, concepts, or processes.

> **Do you UNDERSTAND?**  **MATHEMATICAL PRACTICES**
>
> **3. Writing** Describe how you would determine whether the lengths of the medians from base angles D and F are congruent.
>
> **4. Error Analysis** A student says that the quadrilateral with vertices $D(1, 2)$, $E(0, 7)$, $F(5, 6)$, and $G(7, 0)$
>
>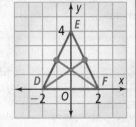

7 LOOK FOR AND MAKE USE OF STRUCTURE.

Mathematically proficient students look closely to discern a pattern or structure. Young students, for example, might notice that three and seven more is the same amount as seven and three more, or they may sort a collection of shapes according to how many sides the shapes have. Later, students will see 7×8 equals the well-remembered $7 \times 5 + 7 \times 3$, in preparation for learning about the distributive property. In the expression $x^2 + 9x + 14$, older students can see the 14 as 2×7 and the 9 as $2 + 7$. They recognize the significance of an existing line in a geometric figure and can use the strategy of drawing an auxiliary line for solving problems. They also can step back for an overview and shift perspective. They can see complicated things, such as some algebraic expressions, as single objects or as being composed of several objects. For example, they can see $5 - 3(x - y)^2$ as 5 minus a positive number times a square, and use that to realize that its value cannot be more than 5 for any real numbers x and y.

Throughout the program, students are encouraged to discern patterns and structures as they look to formulate solution plans. In many of the **Solve Its!,** students are prompted to look within the problem situation for simpler problems to solve.

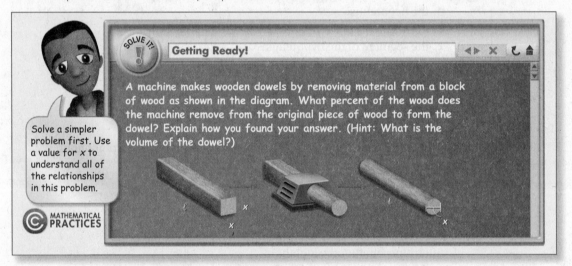

Plan

What values should you choose for x?
Use the same values of x for graphing both functions so that you can see the relationship between corresponding y-coordinates.

Think

Can you use the quadratic formula to solve part (A)?
Yes. You can use the quadratic formula with $a = 3$, $b = 0$, and $c = -9$. However, it is faster to use square roots.

These blue boxes also remind students to think about **the structure of the equation.**

As you work through the lessons, consider asking these questions to help your students develop proficiency with this standard:

- What do the different parts of the expression tell you about possible answers?
- What do you notice about the answers to these exercises?

8 LOOK FOR AND EXPRESS REGULARITY IN REPEATED REASONING.

Mathematically proficient students notice if calculations are repeated, and look both for general methods and for shortcuts. Upper elementary students might notice when dividing 25 by 11 that they are repeating the same calculations over and over again, and conclude they have a repeating decimal. By paying attention to the calculation of slope as they repeatedly check whether points are on the line through (1, 2) with slope 3, middle school students might abstract the equation $(y - 2)/(x - 1) = 3$. Noticing the regularity in the way terms cancel when expanding $(x - 1)(x + 1)$, $(x - 1)(x^2 + x + 1)$, and $(x - 1)(x^3 + x^2 + x + 1)$ might lead them to the general formula for the sum of a geometric series. As they work to solve a problem, mathematically proficient students maintain oversight of the process, while attending to the details. They continually evaluate the reasonableness of their intermediate results.

Through the **Think, Plan** boxes, students are prompted to **look for repetition in calculations** to devise general methods or shortcuts that can make the problem solving process more efficient.

Think

Can you generalize these results?
Yes. All points on a horizontal line have the same *y*-value, so the slope is always zero. Finding the slope of a vertical line always leads to division by zero. The slope is always undefined.

Think

Have you seen a problem like this one?
Yes. Finding percent increase is like finding percent decrease. The difference is in calculating the amount of increase or decrease.

Students are encouraged to think about **similar problems** they solved previously or to **generalize results** to other problem situations.

The **Online Step-by-Step Problems** found at PowerAlgebra.com and PowerGeometry.com, offer students opportunities to **notice regularity** in the way operations or functions behave.

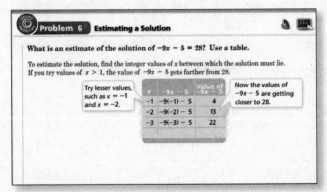

As you work through the lessons, consider asking these questions to help your students develop proficiency with this standard:

- What patterns do you see? Can you make a generalization?
- What relationships do you see in the problem?

Standards for Mathematical Content

The Common Core State Standards for Mathematics (CCSSM) promote a more conceptual and analytical approach to the study of mathematics. In the elementary and middle years, the CCSSM encourage the development of algebraic concepts and skills from students' understanding of arithmetic operations. Students apply their knowledge of place value, properties of operations, and the inverse relationships between operations to write and solve first arithmetic, and then algebraic equations of varying complexities. In the late elementary years, students begin to manipulate parts of the expression and explore the meaning of the expression when it is rewritten in different forms. This early analytic focus helps students look more fully at the equations and expressions so that they begin to see patterns in the structure.

At the high school level, the organization of the standards is by conceptual category. Within each conceptual category, except modeling, content is organized into domains, clusters, and standards. The summaries that follow present the key concepts and progressions for these conceptual categories: Algebra, Number and Quantity, Functions, Geometry, and Statistics and Probability

MODELING

The CCSSM place a specific emphasis on mathematical modeling, both in the Standards for Mathematical Practices and Standards for Mathematical Content. With this focus, the authors of the CCSSM look to highlight the pervasive utility and applicability of mathematical concepts in real-world situations and students' daily lives.

The CCSSM presents a basic modeling cycle that involves a 6-step process: *(1) identifying variables in the situation and selecting those that represent essential features, (2) formulating a model by creating and selecting geometric, graphical, tabular, algebraic, or statistical representations that describe relationships between the variables, (3) analyzing and performing operations on these relationships to draw conclusions, (4) interpreting the results of the mathematics in terms of the original situation, (5) validating the conclusions by comparing them with the situation, and then either improving the model or, if it is acceptable, (6) reporting on the conclusions and the reasoning behind them. Choices, assumptions, and approximations are present throughout this cycle* (CCSSM 2010, 72–73).

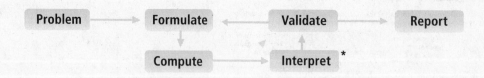

*Common Core State Standards Initiative. Common Core State Standards for Mathematics. Washington, DC. (2010) 72.

NUMBER AND QUANTITY

From the elementary through middle years, students regularly expand their notion of number, from counting to whole numbers, then to fractions, including decimal fractions, and next to negative whole numbers and fractions to form the rational numbers, and finally, by the end of middle years, to irrational numbers to form the real numbers. In high school, students deepen their understanding of the real number system and then come to know the complex number system.

The domains and clusters in this conceptual category are shown below.

The Real Number System
- Extend the properties of exponents to rational exponents.
- Use properties of rational and irrational numbers.

Quantities
- Reason quantitatively and use units to solve problems.

The Complex Number System
- Perform arithmetic operations with complex numbers.
- Represent complex numbers and their operations on the complex plane.
- Use complex numbers in polynomial identities and equations.

Vector and Matrix Quantities
- Represent and model with vector quantities.
- Perform operations on vectors.
- Perform operations on matrices and use matrices in applications.

As students encounter these expanding notions of number, they expand the meanings of addition, subtraction, multiplication, and division while recognizing that the properties of these operations remain constant. Students also realize that the expanded meanings of operations are consistent with their previous meanings.

ALGEBRA

By the end of Grade 8, students have synthesized their knowledge of operations, proportional relationships, and algebraic equations and have begun to formalize their understanding of linearity and linear equations.

The study of algebra in the high school years extends the conceptual and analytic approach of the elementary and middle years. It expands the focus of study from solving equation and applying formulae to include a structural analysis of expressions, equations, and inequalities. The CCSSM domain names and cluster descriptions are a telling indication of this analytic approach.

Seeing Structure in Expressions
- Interpret the structure of expressions.
- Write expressions in equivalent forms to solve problems.

Arithmetic with Polynomials and Rational Functions
- Perform arithmetic operations on polynomials.
- Understand the relationship between zeros and factors of polynomials.
- Use polynomial identities to solve problems.
- Rewrite rational expressions.

Creating Equations
- Create equations that describe numbers or relationships.

Reasoning with Equations and Inequalities
- Understand solving equations as a process of reasoning and explain the reasoning.
- Solve equations and inequalities in one variable.
- Solve systems of equations.
- Represent and solve equations and inequalities graphically.

High school students expand their analysis of linear expressions started in Grade 8 to exponential and quadratic expressions, and then to polynomial and rational expressions. They use their understanding of the structure of expressions and the meaning of each term within expressions to rewrite expressions in equivalent forms to solve problems. Students draw from their understanding of arithmetic operations with numbers to solve algebraic equations and inequalities, including polynomial and rational equations and inequalities.

High school students write equations and inequalities in one or more variables to represent constraints, relationships, and/or numbers. They interpret solutions to equations or inequalities as viable or non-viable options in a modeling context. Students develop fluency using expressions and equations, from linear, exponential, quadratic to polynomial, and rational, including simple root functions. They represent expressions and equations graphically, starting with linear, exponential, and quadratic equations and progressing to polynomial, rational, and radical equations.

High school students come to understand the process of solving equations as one of reasoning. They construct viable arguments to justify a solution method. In advanced algebra courses, students explain the presence and meaning of extraneous solutions in some solutions sets.

FUNCTIONS

Students began a formal study of functions in Grade 8 where they explored functions presented in different ways (algebraically, numerically in tables, and graphically) and compared the properties of different functions presented in different ways. They described the functional relationship between two quantities and represented the relationship graphically.

The domains and clusters for Functions are listed below.

Interpreting Functions
- Understand the concept of a function and use function notation.
- Interpret functions that arise in applications in terms of the context.
- Analyze functions using different representations.

Building Functions
- Build a function that models a relationship between two quantities.
- Build new functions from existing functions.

Linear, Quadratic, and Exponential Models
- Construct and compare linear and exponential models and solve problems.
- Interpret expressions for functions in terms of the situation they model.

Trigonometric Functions
- Extend the domain of trigonometric functions using the unit circle.
- Model periodic phenomena with trigonometric functions.
- Prove and apply trigonometric identities.

Building on their knowledge of functions, high school students use function notation to express linear and exponential functions, and arithmetic and geometric sequences. They also compare properties of two (or more) functions, each represented algebraically, graphically, numerically using tables, or by verbal description, and describe the common effect of each transformation across different types of functions. They analyze progressively more complex functions, from linear, exponential, and quadratic to absolute value, step, and piecewise functions.

A strong emphasis in the study of functions is its applicability to real-world situations and relationships. Students build functions that model real-world situations and/or relationships, including simple radical, rational, and exponential functions. They also interpret linear, exponential, and quadratic functions in real-world situations and applications. More advanced study of functions includes trigonometric functions. Students extend the domain of trigonometric functions using the unit circle and model periodic phenomena with trigonometric functions. They also prove and apply trigonometric identities.

GEOMETRY

In high school geometry, students expand their experiences with transformations and engage in formal proofs of geometric theorems, using transformations in the plane as a foundation to prove congruence and similarity. From this foundation, students look to define trigonometric ratios and apply these concepts to solve problems involving right triangles.

In the middle years, students undertook an exploration of congruence and similarity through transformations. They verified the properties of transformations (reflections, translations, rotations, dilations) and described the effect of each on two-dimensional shapes using coordinates. Student explained that shapes are congruent or similar based on a sequence of transformations.

Listed are the domains and clusters for Geometry.

Congruence
- Experiment with transformations in the plane.
- Understand congruence in terms of rigid motions.
- Prove geometric theorems.
- Make geometric constructions.

Similarity, Right Triangles, and Trigonometry
- Understand similarity in terms of similarity transformations.
- Prove theorems involving similarity.
- Define trigonometric ratios and solve problems involving right triangles.
- Apply trigonometry to general triangles.

Circles
- Understand and apply theorems about circles.
- Find arc lengths and areas of sectors of circles.

Expressing Geometric Properties with Equations
- Translate between the geometric description and the equation for a conic section.
- Use coordinates to prove simple geometric theorems algebraically.

Geometric Measurement and Dimension
- Explain volume formulas and use them to solve problems.
- Visualize relationships between two-dimensional and three-dimensional objects.

Modeling with Geometry
- Apply geometric concepts in modeling situations.

High school students engage in a formal study of circles, applying theorems about circles and solving problems related to parts of circles or properties of circles. Through the study of equations that describe geometric shapes, students connect algebraic manipulation of equations or formulae to geometric properties and structures. As with other mathematical concepts, students investigate modeling real-world situations or relationships by applying geometric concepts.

STATISTICS AND PROBABILITY

The Common Core State Standards put more emphasis on interpreting data in both measurement and quantitative variables. Students are expected to evaluate random processes and justify conclusions from sample surveys and experiments. Conditional probability and probability of compound events are used to interpret data.

In the middle years, students began an exploration of statistics. They looked at measures of center and measures of variability to understand the visual representation of data sets and to analyze the attributes of a data set based on its visual representation. In Grade 8, students analyzed representations of bivariate data.

The domains and clusters for Statistics and Probability are shown below.

Interpreting Categorical and Quantitative Data
- Summarize, represent, and interpret data on a single count or measurement variable.
- Summarize, represent, and interpret data on two categorical and quantitative variables.
- Interpret linear models.

Making Inferences and Justifying Conclusions
- Understand and evaluate random processes underlying statistical experiments.
- Make inferences and justify conclusions from sample surveys, experiments and observational studies.

Conditional Probability and the Rules of Probability
- Understand independence and conditional probability and use them to interpret data.
- Use the rules of probability to compute probabilities of compound events in a uniform probability model.

Using Probability to Make Decisions
- Calculate expected values and use them to solve problems.
- Use probability to evaluate outcomes of decisions.

In high school, students expand on their understanding of statistics and data representations to interpret data on a single variable and on two categorical and quantitative variables.

High school students work with frequency tables, including joint marginal and conditional relative frequencies. They practice determining the best metric for reporting data. Students learn that statistics is a process for making inferences about a population based on a random sample from that population. They determine which statistical model is best for a given set of data. Students spend time using tools such as calculators, spreadsheets and tables to examine their data. They work with the population mean and the margin of error to understand the limitations of statistical models. They look at probability models to analyze decisions and make predictions.

Assessing the Common Core State Standards

The adoption and implementation of the Common Core State Standards for Mathematics is an important and critical step to improving students' math achievement in the United States. A second, equally important step is creating assessments grounded in these standards to measure students' progress against these new standards. These common assessments can also ensure that all students have access to these new standards.

The Race to the Top Assessment Program, funded by the American Recovery and Reinvestment Act of 2009 (ARRA) awarded funding to two state consortia to **develop next generation assessment and accountability systems.** These valid and reliable assessments will be used to measure students' progress against the Common Core State Standards, provide a common measure of college and career readiness, and make use of new technologies in assessment and reporting so that parents and teachers have timely information about student performance.

> These common assessments can also ensure that *all* students have access to these new standards.

These next generation assessment systems, which are to be operational by 2014–2015, are to meet the dual needs of accountability and instructional improvement. With these common assessments, state and local school officials can get an accurate view of how their students' performances compare to those of students in other districts or states. They can also reduce challenges associated with student mobility. Students in over 40 states will be expected to learn the same content and will take the same or similar assessments.

These new assessments will focus on assessing the critical areas that the Common Core State Standards identified for each grade from Kindergarten through Grade 8. These assessments will also include tasks to measure students' mathematical proficiency as described in the Standards for Mathematical Practice.

The two state consortia are the **Partnership for Assessment of Readiness for College and Careers** (PARCC) and the **SMARTER Balanced Assessment Consortium** (SBAC).

On the following page are brief descriptions of the assessments plans for PARCC and SBAC.

Partnership for Assessment of Readiness for College and Careers

The Partnership for Assessment of Readiness for College and Careers Consortium (PARCC) is made up of 24 states and the District of Columbia. The consortium is working with Achieve Inc., an independent, bipartisan, non-profit education reform organization, and more than 200 colleges or universities to develop its next generation assessment system.

The PARCC assessment system will be made up of a series of summative assessments given throughout the school year. The summative assessment will have three Through-Course Assessments and one End-of-Year Comprehensive Assessment.

The **Through-Course Assessments** will be given towards the end of the first, second, and third quarters and will focus on the critical areas for each course. Assessing these areas closer to the time of instruction allows for mid-year corrections as needed.

- The first and second Through-Course Assessment will require one class period to complete. The third Through-Course Assessment may require more than one class period to complete.
- Students will take these assessments primarily on computers or other digital devices. They will encounter a range of item types, including performance tasks and computer-enhanced items.
- The scoring for these assessments will be a combination of computer-scored and human-scored. The results will be reported within a few weeks of administration.

The **End-of-Year Assessment** will assess all of the standards at the grade level. It will measure students' conceptual understanding, procedural fluency, and problem solving.

- It will be taken online during the last 4 to 6 weeks of the school year.
- It will have 40 to 65 items, with a range of item types (i.e., selected-response, constructed-response, performance tasks) and cognitive demand.
- It will be entirely computer-scored

A student's score will be based on his or her scores on the three Through-Course Assessments and the End-of-Year Assessment. This score will be used for the purposes of accountability.

PARCC will also make available aligned formative assessments that teachers can use in the classroom throughout the school year.

SMARTER Balanced Assessment Consortium

The SMARTER Balanced Assessment Consortium (SBAC) is made up of 31 states. The fiscal agent for the consortium is Washington state. The consortium is working with WestEd, a nonprofit, public research and development agency, and more than 170 colleges and universities to develop its next generation assessment system.

The SBAC assessment system will consist of Performance Tasks and an End-of-Year Adaptive Assessment.

Students will complete two Performance Tasks during the last 12 weeks of the school year. These tasks will measure students' abilities to integrate knowledge and skills from the Common Core State Standards for Mathematics.

- Students will take these assessments primarily on computers or other digital devices.
- Each task will take one or two class periods to complete.
- The tasks will involve student-initiated planning, interaction with other materials, and production of extended responses.
- The tasks will be scored by both computers and humans.
- Results will be available as soon as possible.

The **End-of-Year Assessment** will use computer-adaptive delivery so that the scores accurately reflect student achievement.

- it will be administered during the last 12 weeks of the school year.
- It will be made up of 40 to 65 items, with a range of item types (i.e., selected-response, constructed-response, technology-enhanced).
- Some items will be computer scored while others will be human scored.
- Some students may be approved for a re-take with a new set of items.

A student's score will be based on his or her scores on the Performance Tasks and the End-of-Year Adaptive Assessment. This score will be used for the purposes of accountability.

SBAC will also make available an optional system of computer-adaptive interim assessments whose uses can be customized by local districts or schools. These assessments will have items similar to those on the End-of-Year Assessment. The report of student results will also identify appropriate student resources based on student performance.

Standards for Mathematical Practice
Observational Protocol

Name of Student	Dates of Observations			
Suggested rating: P = shows proficiency; D= developing; E = emerging; O = No evidence				

1. Make sense of problems and persevere in solving them.				

a. identifies main task of the problem	e. checks reasonableness of solution
b. relates to other problems	f. checks solution plans
c. explains relationships among numbers or quantities	g. uses a different method to check solution
d. identifies solution plan	h. compares/contrasts solution plan

NOTES

2. Reason abstractly and quantitatively				

a. explains relationships among numbers	c. explains referents and meaning of numbers
b. writes an equation or expression for a problem	d. explains meaning of quantities

NOTES

3. Construct viable arguments and critique the reasoning of others.				

a. asks appropriate questions	c. explains solution and justifies conclusions
b. compares and contrasts various solutions	d. recognizes flaws in logic/thinking

NOTES

4. Model with mathematics.				

a. represents a problem situation	d. analyses relationships of quantities
b. identifies the key quantities	e. explains relationships among quantities
c. represents relationships among quantities graphically	f. asks whether the solution is reasonable

NOTES

Name of Student	Dates of Obseravtions			

5. Use appropriate tools strategically.				

a. describes possible uses of tools, technology

b. selects most helpful tools

c. uses technology tools appropriately

d. identifies possible errors using estimation

e. explains advantages and limitations of different tools

NOTES

6. Attend to precision.				

a. states the meaning of symbols used

b. uses precise definitions

c. specifies units of measure

d. calculates accurately

e. uses precise language to explain solutions and justify conclusions

NOTES

7. Look for and make use of structure				

a. notices a pattern or structure in expressions or equations

b. recognizes a pattern in the solutions of problems

NOTES

8. Look for and express regularity in repeated reasoning.				

a. notices repeated calculation or methods

b. derives general methods or shortcuts from repeated calculations

NOTES

Dear Parents

Recently, more than 40 states in the Unites States have developed and adopted a common set of academic standards in mathematics. These standards, called the **Common Core State Standards** were developed in collaboration with teachers, school administrators, and mathematics and education experts under the auspices of the National Governors' Association and the Council for Chief State School Officers (CCSSO).

These standards will serve as important benchmarks to ensure that **all students are receiving high quality education and are well prepared for success in post-secondary education and the workforce.** Students will be assessed on a regular basis throughout their school career to monitor their progress towards meeting these benchmarks.

As individual states have adopted these new standards, they have committed to a shared grade-by-grade sequence of topics to be taught. For many states, this requires a shift in the instructional materials used, to match both the content skills and the mathematical understandings contained in the Common Core State Standards.

Your son·or daughter is using *Pearson High School Mathematics Common Core Edition* ©2012 in his/her math·course. **This program was specially developed to provide comprehensive coverage of the Common Core State Standards for Mathematics.** Take a look through your son or daughter's math textbook and you'll notice that each lesson specifically targets one or more of the content standards (shown to the right of the lesson title). You'll find a listing of all of the content standards addressed in the course on pages xvi through xix.

You'll also notice that many of the problems and exercises in the lessons have a red logo next to them. While all of the problems and exercises in the program support students in deepening their math understanding and content knowledge, these exercises highlight particular opportunities for you child to develop the mathematical skills and habits of mind that are part of the Common Core State Standards. Called the **Standards for Mathematical Practices,** these standards describe practices and abilities of very good math thinkers. You can help your son or daughter develop these abilities by asking the questions found on the back of this letter as they work on homework assignments.

Pearson is committed to providing quality instructional materials that can help all students achieve mastery of the Common Core State Standards and be well prepared for success after high school. We hope that your child has a successful and rewarding year in the study of mathematics!

Sincerely,

Standards for Mathematical Practice
Parents' Guide

As your son or daughter works through homework exercises, you can help him or her develop skill with these standards by asking some of these questions:

1. **Make sense of problems and persevere in solving them.**
   - What is the problem that you are solving for?
   - Can you think of a problem that you recently solved that is similar to this one?
   - How will you go about solving the problem? (i.e., What's your plan?)
   - Are you progressing towards a solution? Should you try a different solution plan?
   - How can you check your solution using a different method?

2. **Construct viable arguments and critique the reasoning of others.**
   - Can you write or recall an expression or equation to match the problem situation?
   - What do the numbers or variables in the equation refer to?
   - What's the connection among the numbers and variables in the equation?

3. **Reason abstractly and quantitatively.**
   - Tell me what your answers means.
   - How do you know that your answer is correct?
   - If I told you I think the answer should be [a wrong answer], how would you explain to me why I'm wrong?

4. **Model with mathematics.**
   - Do you know a formula or relationship that fits this problem situation?
   - What's the connection among the numbers in the problem?
   - Is your answer reasonable? How do you know?
   - What do(es) the number(s) in your solution refer to?

5. **Use appropriate tools strategically.**
   - What tools could you use to solve this problem? How can each one help you?
   - Which tool is more useful for this problem? Explain your choice.
   - Why is this tool (the one selected) better to use than [another tool mentioned]?
   - Before you solve the problem, can you estimate the solution?

6. **Reason abstractly and quantitatively.**
   - What do the symbols that you used mean?
   - What units of measure are you using? (for measurement problems)
   - Explain to me what is [term from the lesson].

7. **Look for and make use of structure.**
   - What do you notice about the answers to the exercises you've just completed?
   - What do different parts of the expression or equation you are using tell you about possible correct answers?

8. **Look for and express regularity in repeated reasoning.**
   - What shortcut can you think of that will always work for these kinds of problems?
   - What pattern(s) do you see? Can you make a generalization?

Standards for Mathematical Content for High School

Following is a correlation of *Pearson High School Mathematics Common Core Edition* ©2012 to the Standards for Mathematical Content in the Common Core State Standards for High School Mathematics. The standards with (+) indicate additional mathematics that students should learn in order to take advanced courses such as calculus, advanced statistics, or discrete mathematics. Most of these standards are generally addressed in a 4th year mathematics course, although as is shown in this document, a number of these standards are addressed in *Pearson High School Mathematics Common Core Program*. Standards with a star (*) are modeling standards.

Number and Quantity		Where to find
The Real Number System		**N.RN**
Extend the properties of exponents to rational exponents		
N.RN.1	Explain how the definition of the meaning of rational exponents follows from extending the properties of integer exponents to those values, allowing for a notation for radicals in terms of rational exponents.	Algebra 1: 7-2, 7-3, 7-4
N.RN.2	Rewrite expressions involving radicals and rational exponents using the properties of exponents.	Algebra 1: 7-5
Use properties of rational and irrational numbers.		
N.RN.3	Explain why the sum or product of two rational numbers is rational, that the sum of a rational number and an irrational number is irrational, and that the product of a nonzero rational number and an irrational number is irrational.	Algebra 1: CB 1-6
Quantities		**N.Q**
Reason quantitatively and use units to solve problems		
N.Q.1	Use units as a way to understand problems and to guide the solution of multi-step problems; choose and interpret units consistently in formulas; choose and interpret the scale and the origin in graphs and data displays.	Algebra 1: 2-5, 2-6, CB 2-6, 2-7, 4-4, 5-7, 12-2, 12-4 Geometry: 1-8
N.Q.2	Define appropriate quantities for the purpose of descriptive modeling.	Algebra 1: 2-6, CB 2-6, 3-3, 4-5, 5-2, 5-5, 6-4, 9-3, 12-3
N.Q.3	Choose a level of accuracy appropriate to limitations on measurement when reporting quantities.	Algebra 1: 2-10, 6-4, 9-5, 9-6
The Complex Number System		**N.CN**
Perform arithmetic operations with complex numbers		
N.CN.1	Know there is a complex number i such that $i^2 = -1$, and every complex number has the form $a + bi$ with a and b real.	Algebra 2: 4-8
N.CN.2	Use the relation $i^2 = -1$ and the commutative, associative, and distributive properties to add, subtract, and multiply complex numbers.	Algebra 2: 4-8
N.CN.3	(+) Find the conjugate of a complex number; use conjugates to find moduli and quotients of complex numbers.	Studied in a 4th year course

Number and Quantity		Where to find
Represent complex numbers and their operations on the complex plane		
N.CN.4	(+) Represent complex numbers on the complex plane in rectangular and polar form (including real and imaginary numbers), and explain why the rectangular and polar forms of a given complex number represent the same number.	Studied in a 4th year course
N.CN.5	(+) Represent addition, subtraction, multiplication, and conjugation of complex numbers geometrically on the complex plane; use properties of this representation for computation.	Studied in a 4th year course
N.CN.6	(+) Calculate the distance between numbers in the complex plane as the modulus of the difference, and the midpoint of a segment as the average of the numbers at its endpoints.	Studied in a 4th year course
Use complex numbers in polynomial identities and equations		
N.CN.7	Solve quadratic equations with real coefficients that have complex solutions.	Algebra 2: 4-8, 5-5, 5-6
N.CN.8	(+) Extend polynomial identities to the complex numbers.	Algebra 2: 4-8, 5-5, 5-6
N.CN.9	(+) Know the Fundamental Theorem of Algebra; show that it is true for quadratic polynomials.	Algebra 2: 5-6
Vector and Matrix Quantities		**N.VM**
Represent and model with vector quantities		
N.VM.1	(+) Recognize vector quantities as having both magnitude and direction. Represent vector quantities by directed line segments, and use appropriate symbols for vectors and their magnitudes (e.g., $\mathbf{v}$, $|\mathbf{v}|$, $\|\mathbf{v}\|$, v).	Algebra 2: 12-6
N.VM.2	(+) Find the components of a vector by subtracting the coordinates of an initial point from the coordinates of a terminal point.	Algebra 2: 12-6
N.VM.3	(+) Solve problems involving velocity and other quantities that can be represented by vectors.	Algebra 2: 12-6
Perform operations on vectors		
N.VM.4	(+) Add and subtract vectors.	Algebra 2: 12-6
N.VM.4.a	Add vectors end-to-end, component-wise, and by the parallelogram rule. Understand that the magnitude of a sum of two vectors is typically not the sum of the magnitudes.	Algebra 2: 12-6
N.VM.4.b	Given two vectors in magnitude and direction form, determine the magnitude and direction of their sum.	Algebra 2: 12-6
N.VM.4.c	Understand vector subtraction $\mathbf{v} - \mathbf{w}$ as $\mathbf{v} + (-\mathbf{w})$, where $-\mathbf{w}$ is the additive inverse of $\mathbf{w}$, with the same magnitude as $\mathbf{w}$ and pointing in the opposite direction. Represent vector subtraction graphically by connecting the tips in the appropriate order, and perform vector subtraction component-wise.	Algebra 2: 12-6
N.VM.5	(+) Multiply a vector by a scalar.	Algebra 2: 12-6
N.VM.5.a	Represent scalar multiplication graphically by scaling vectors and possibly reversing their direction; perform scalar multiplication component-wise, e.g., as $c(v_x, v_y) = (cv_x, cv_y)$.	Algebra 2: 12-6
N.VM.5.b	Compute the magnitude of a scalar multiple $c\mathbf{v}$ using $\|c\mathbf{v}\| = |c|v$. Compute the direction of $c\mathbf{v}$ knowing that when $|c|v \neq 0$, the direction of $c\mathbf{v}$ is either along $\mathbf{v}$ (for $c > 0$) or against $\mathbf{v}$ (for $c < 0$).	Algebra 2: 12-6

Number and Quantity		Where to find
Perform operations on matrices and use matrices in applications		
N.VM.6	(+) Use matrices to represent and manipulate data, e.g., to represent payoffs or incidence relationships in a network.	Algebra 2: 12-2, 12-5, CB 12-2
N.VM.7	(+) Multiply matrices by scalars to produce new matrices, e.g., as when all of the payoffs in a game are doubled.	Algebra 2: 12-2, 12-5
N.VM.8	(+) Add, subtract, and multiply matrices of appropriate dimensions.	Algebra 2: 12-1, 12-2, 12-4, 12-5, CB 12-1
N.VM.9	(+) Understand that, unlike multiplication of numbers, matrix multiplication for square matrices is not a commutative operation, but still satisfies the associative and distributive properties.	Algebra 2: 12-2
N.VM.10	(+) Understand that the zero and identity matrices play a role in matrix addition and multiplication similar to the role of 0 and 1 in the real numbers. The determinant of a square matrix is nonzero if and only if the matrix has a multiplicative inverse.	Algebra 2: 12-1, 12-3
N.VM.11	(+) Multiply a vector (regarded as a matrix with one column) by a matrix of suitable dimensions to produce another vector. Work with matrices as transformations of vectors.	Algebra 2: 12-6
N.VM.12	(+) Work with 2 × 2 matrices as transformations of the plane, and interpret the absolute value of the determinant in terms of area.	Algebra 2: 12-3, 12-6

Algebra	Where to find

Seeing Structure in Expressions   **A.SSE**

Interpret the structure of expressions

A.SSE.1	Interpret expressions that represent a quantity in terms of its context.*	Algebra 1: 1-1, 1-2, 3-7, 4-5, 4-7, 5-3, 5-4, 5-5, 7-6, 7-7, 7-8, 8-7, 8-8, 9-1, 9-2, 9-5, 9-6 Algebra 2: 5-2, 8-4
A.SSE.1.a	Interpret parts of an expression, such as terms, factors, and coefficients.	Algebra 1: 1-1, 1-2, 1-7, 4-5, 4-7, 5-3, 5-4, 7-7, 7-8, 8-5, 8-6, 8-7, 8-8, 9-5 Algebra 2: 4-5, 5-1, 8-4
A.SSE.1.b	Interpret complicated expressions by viewing one or more of their parts as a single entity.	Algebra 1: 3-7, 4-7, 7-7, 8-6, 8-7, 8-8, 9-5 Algebra 2: 1-6, 7-1, 7-2, 7-3, 8-4
A.SSE.2	Use the structure of an expression to identify ways to rewrite it.	Algebra 1: 5-3, 5-4, 5-5, 8-7, 8-8 Algebra 2: 4-4, 5-3, 6-1, 6-2, 6-3, 8-4

Write expressions in equivalent forms to solve problems

A.SSE.3	Choose and produce an equivalent form of an expression to reveal and explain properties of the quantity represented by the expression.	Algebra 1: 9-4, 9-5
A.SSE.3.a	Factor a quadratic expression to reveal the zeros of the function it defines.	Algebra 1: 9-4
A.SSE.3.b	Complete the square in a quadratic expression to reveal the maximum or minimum value of the function it defines.	Algebra 1: 9-5
A.SSE.3.c	Use the properties of exponents to transform expressions for exponential functions.	Algebra 1: 7-7
A.SSE.4	Derive the formula for the sum of a finite geometric series (when the common ratio is not 1), and use the formula to solve problems.	Algebra 2: 9-5, CB 9-5

Arithmetic with Polynomials and Rational Expressions   **A.APR**

Perform arithmetic operations on polynomials

A.APR.1	Understand that polynomials form a system analogous to the integers, namely, they are closed under the operations of addition, subtraction, and multiplication; add, subtract, and multiply polynomials.	Algebra 1: 8-1, 8-2, 8-3, 8-4 Algebra 2: 5-4

Understand the relationship between zeros and factors of polynomial

A.APR.2	Know and apply the Remainder Theorem: For a polynomial $p(x)$ and a number a, the remainder on division by $x - a$ is $p(a)$, so $p(a) = 0$ if and only if $(x - a)$ is a factor of $p(x)$.	Algebra 2: 5-4
A.APR. 3	Identify zeros of polynomials when suitable factorizations are available, and use the zeros to construct a rough graph of the function defined by the polynomial.	Algebra 1: 9-3, CB 9-3 Algebra 2: 4-5, 5-2, 5-6, CB 5-7

Algebra	Where to find

Use polynomial identities to solve problems

A.APR.4	• Prove polynomial identities and use them to describe numerical relationships.	Algebra 2: CB 5-5
A.APR.5	(+) Know and apply the Binomial Theorem for the expansion of $(x + y)^n$ in powers of x and y for a positive integer n, where x and y are any numbers, with coefficients determined for example by Pascal's Triangle. (Note: The Binomial Theorem can be proved by mathematical induction or by a combinatorial argument.)	Algebra 2: 5-7

Rewrite rational expressions

A.APR.6	Rewrite simple rational expressions in different forms; write $\frac{a(x)}{b(x)}$ in the form $q(x) + \frac{r(x)}{b(x)}$, where $a(x)$, $b(x)$, $q(x)$, and $r(x)$ are polynomials with the degree of $r(x)$ less than the degree of $b(x)$, using inspection, long division, or, for the more complicated examples, a computer algebra system.	Algebra 1: 11-3 Algebra 2: 5-4, 8-6
A.APR.7	(+) Understand that rational expressions form a system analogous to the rational numbers, closed under addition, subtraction, multiplication, and division by a nonzero rational expression; add, subtract, multiply, and divide rational expressions.	Algebra 1: 11-2, 11-4 Algebra 2: 8-5, 8-6

Creating Equations★   A.CED

Create equations that describe numbers or relationships

A.CED.1	Create equations and inequalities in one variable and use them to solve problems. *Include equations arising from linear and quadratic functions, and simple rational and exponential functions.*	Algebra 1: 1-8, 2-1, 2-2, 2-3, 2-4, 2-5, 2-7, 2-8, 3-2, 3-3, 3-4, 3-6, 3-7, 3-8, 9-3, 9-4, 9-5, 9-6, 11-5 Algebra 2: 1-4, 1-5, 1-6, 4-1, 4-5, CB 8-1, 8-6
A.CED.2	Create equations in two or more variables to represent relationships between quantities; graph equations on coordinate axes with labels and scales.	Algebra 1: 1-9, 4-5, 5-2, 5-3, 5-4, 5-5, 7-6, 7-7, 9-1, 9-2, CB 9-4, 10-5, 11-6, 11-7, CB 11-7 Algebra 2: 2-2, 2-3, 2-4, 2-5, 2-8, 3-1, 3-2, 4-2, CB 4-5, 7-1, 7-2, 8-1, 8-2, 8-3
A.CED.3	Represent constraints by equations or inequalities, and by systems of equations and/or inequalities, and interpret solutions as viable or non-viable options in a modeling context.	Algebra 1: 6-4, 6-5, 9-8 Algebra 2: 3-1, 3-2, 3-3, 3-4, CB 3-4, 4-9, CB 7-6
A.CED.4	Rearrange formulas to highlight a quantity of interest, using the same reasoning as in solving equations.	Algebra 1: 2-5, 9-3 Algebra 2: 1-4, 6-5, 8-1

Algebra	Where to find
Reasoning with Equations and Inequalities	**A.REI**

Understand solving equations as a process of reasoning and explain the reasoning

A.REI.1	Explain each step in solving a simple equation as following from the equality of numbers asserted at the previous step, starting from the assumption that the original equation has a solution. Construct a viable argument to justify a solution method.	Algebra 1: 2-2, 2-3, 2-4, 2-5, 9-5
A.REI.2	Solve simple rational and radical equations in one variable, and give examples showing how extraneous solutions may arise.	Algebra 1: 10-4, 11-5 Algebra 2: 6-5, 8-6

Solve equations and inequalities in one variable

A.REI.3	Solve linear equations and inequalities in one variable, including equations with coefficients represented by letters.	Algebra 1: 2-1, 2-2, 2-3, 2-4, 2-5, 2-7, 2-8, 3-2, 3-3, 3-4, 3-5, 3-6
A.REI.4	Solve quadratic equations in one variable.	Algebra 1: 9-3, 9-4, 9-5, 9-6
A.REI.4.a	Use the method of completing the square to transform any quadratic equation in x into an equation of the form $(x - p)^2 = q$ that has the same solutions. Derive the quadratic formula from this form.	Algebra 1: 9-5, 9-6
A.REI.4.b	Solve quadratic equations by inspection (e.g., for $x^2 = 49$), taking square roots, completing the square, the quadratic formula and factoring, as appropriate to the initial form of the equation. Recognize when the quadratic formula gives complex solutions and write them as $a \pm bi$ for real numbers a and b.	Algebra 1: 9-3, 9-4, 9-5, 9-6

Solve systems of equations

A.REI.5	Prove that, given a system of two equations in two variables, replacing one equation by the sum of that equation and a multiple of the other produces a system with the same solutions.	Algebra 1: 6-3 Algebra 2: 3-2
A.REI.6	Solve systems of linear equations exactly and approximately (e.g., with graphs), focusing on pairs of linear equations in two variables.	Algebra 1: 6-1, 6-2, 6-3, 6-4 Algebra 2: 3-1, 3-2, 3-3
A.REI.7	Solve a simple system consisting of a linear equation and a quadratic equation in two variables algebraically and graphically.	Algebra 1: 9-8 Algebra 2: 4-9
A.REI.8	(+) Represent a system of linear equations as a single matrix equation in a vector variable.	Algebra 2: 3-6
A.REI.9	(+) Find the inverse of a matrix if it exists and use it to solve systems of linear equations (using technology for matrices of dimension 3×3 or greater).	Studied in 4th year course

Represent and solve equations and inequalities graphically

A.REI.10	Understand that the graph of an equation in two variables is the set of all its solutions plotted in the coordinate plane, often forming a curve (which could be a straight line).	Algebra 1: 1-9, 4-2, 4-3, 4-4
A.REI.11	Explain why the x-coordinates of the points where the graphs of the equations $y = f(x)$ and $y = g(x)$ intersect are the solutions of the equation $f(x) = g(x)$; find the solutions approximately, e.g., using technology to graph the functions, make tables of values, or find successive approximations. Include cases where $f(x)$ and/or $g(x)$ are linear, polynomial, rational, absolute value, exponential, and logarithmic functions.*	Algebra 1: CB 4-4, CB 6-1, 7-6, 9-8 Algebra 2: 3-1, 5-3, 7-5, CB 7-6, 8-6

Algebra		Where to find
Functions		
A.REI.12	Graph the solutions to a linear inequality in two variables as a half-plane (excluding the boundary in the case of a strict inequality), and graph the solution set to a system of linear inequalities in two variables as the intersection of the corresponding half-planes.	Algebra 1: 6-5, 6-6, CB 6-6 Algebra 2: 3-3

Functions		Where to find
Interpreting Functions		**F.IF**
Understand the concept of a function and use function notation		
F.IF.1	Understand that a function from one set (called the domain) to another set (called the range) assigns to each element of the domain exactly one element of the range. If f is a function and x is an element of its domain, then $f(x)$ denotes the output of f corresponding to the input x. The graph of f is the graph of the equation $y = f(x)$.	Algebra 1: 4-6 Algebra 2: 2-2
F.IF.2	Use function notation, evaluate functions for inputs in their domains, and interpret statements that use function notation in terms of a context.	Algebra 1: 4-6
F.IF.3	Recognize that sequences are functions, sometimes defined recursively, whose domain is a subset of the integers.	Algebra 1: 4-7, 7-8 Algebra 2: 9-2, 9-3
Interpret functions that arise in applications in terms of the context		
F.IF.4	For a function that models a relationship between two quantities, interpret key features of graphs and tables in terms of the quantities, and sketch graphs showing key features given a verbal description of the relationship. *Key features include: intercepts; intervals where the function is increasing, decreasing, positive, or negative; relative maximums and minimums; symmetries; end behavior; and periodicity.**	Algebra 1: 4-2, 4-3, 5-3, 5-4, 5-5, 7-6, 7-7, 9-1, 9-2, 9-7, 11-7 Algebra 2: 2-3, 2-5, 4-1, 4-2, 4-3, 5-1, 5-8, CB 7-3, 13-1, 13-4, 13-5
F.IF.5	Relate the domain of a function to its graph and, where applicable, to the quantitative relationship it describes.*	Algebra 1: 4-4, 7-6, 9-1, 11-6 Algebra 2: 4-3, 5-8
F.IF.6	Calculate and interpret the average rate of change of a function (presented symbolically or as a table) over a specified interval. Estimate the rate of change from a graph.*	Algebra 1: 5-1, CB 9-2 Algebra 2: 2-5, 4-1, 4-2, CB 4-3, 5-8
Analyze functions using different representations		
F.IF.7	Graph functions expressed symbolically and show key features of the graph, by hand in simple cases and using technology for more complicated cases.*	Algebra 1: 5-3, 5-4, 5-5, 5-8, 7-6, 7-7, 9-1, 9-2 Algebra 2: 2-3, 2-4, CB 2-4, 2-6, 2-7, 4-1, 4-2, 5-1, 5-2, 5-8, 6-8, 7-2, CB 8-2, CB 8-3
F.IF.7.a	Graph linear and quadratic functions and show intercepts, maxima, and minima.	Algebra 1: 5-3, 5-4, 5-5, 9-1, 9-2

Functions		Where to find
F.IF.7.b	Graph square root, cube root, and piecewise-defined functions, including step functions and absolute value functions.	Algebra 1: 5-8, CB 5-8, 9-1, 10-5
		Algebra 2: CB 2-4, 2-7, 2-8, 6-8
F.IF.7.c	Graph polynomial functions, identifying zeros when suitable factorizations are available, and showing end behavior.	Algebra 2: 5-1, 5-2, 5-9
F.IF.7.d	(+) Graph rational functions, identifying zeros and asymptotes when suitable factorizations are available, and showing end behavior.	Algebra 2: CB 8-2
F.IF.7.e	Graph exponential and logarithmic functions, showing intercepts and end behavior, and trigonometric functions, showing period, midline, and amplitude.	Algebra 2: 7-1, 7-2, 7-3, 13-4, 13-5, 13-6, 13-7, 13-8, CB 7-5
F.IF.8	Write a function defined by an expression in different but equivalent forms to reveal and explain different properties of the function.	Algebra 1: 7-7
		Algebra 2: 2-4, 4-2, 5-9, 6-8, 7-2, 7-3, 10-6, CB 7-5
F.IF.8.a	Use the process of factoring and completing the square in a quadratic function to show zeros, extreme values, and symmetry of the graph, and interpret these in terms of a context.	Algebra 1: 9-4, 9-5
F.IF.8.b	Use the properties of exponents to interpret expressions for exponential functions.	Algebra 1: 7-7
F.IF.9	Compare properties of two functions each represented in a different way (algebraically, graphically, numerically in tables, or by verbal descriptions).	Algebra 1: 5-5, 7-6, 9-2
		Algebra 2: 2-4, 4-2, 5-9, 7-3

Building Functions — F.BF

Build a function that models a relationship between two quantities

F.BF.1	Write a function that describes a relationship between two quantities.*	Algebra 1: 4-7, 5-3, 5-4, 5-5, 7-7, 9-2
		Algebra 2: 2-2, 2-5, 4-2, 5-2, 6-6, 7-2, 8-2, 8-3
F.BF.1.a	Determine an explicit expression, a recursive process, or steps for calculation from a context.	Algebra 1: 4-7, 5-3, 5-4, 5-5, 7-8
F.BF.1.b	Combine standard function types using arithmetic operations.	Algebra 1: 9-7
		Algebra 2: 6-6, 7-2, 8-3
F.BF.1.c	(+) Compose functions.	Algebra 2: 6-6
F.BF.2	Write arithmetic and geometric sequences both recursively and with an explicit formula, use them to model situations, and translate between the two forms.*	Algebra 1: 4-7, 7-8

Build new functions from existing functions

F.BF.3	Identify the effect on the graph of replacing $f(x)$ by $f(x) + k$, $k\,f(x)$, $f(kx)$, and $f(x + k)$ for specific values of k (both positive and negative); find the value of k given the graphs. Experiment with cases and illustrate an explanation of the effects on the graph using technology. *Include recognizing even and odd functions from their graphs and algebraic expressions for them.*	Algebra 1: 5-3, 5-4, 5-8, 7-7, 9-1, 9-2, CB 5-3
		Algebra 2: 2-6, 2-7, 4-1, 5-9, 8-2

Functions		Where to find
F.BF.4	Find inverse functions.	Algebra 1: CB 5-5 Algebra 2: 6-7, 7-3
F.BF.4.a	Solve an equation of the form $f(x) = c$ for a simple function f that has an inverse and write an expression for the inverse.	Algebra 1: CB 5-5 Algebra 2: 6-7, 7-3
F.BF.4.b	(+) Verify by composition that one function is the inverse of another.	Studied in 4th year course
F.BF.4.c	(+) Read values of an inverse function from a graph or a table, given that the function has an inverse.	Algebra 2: 6-7
F.BF.4.d	(+) Produce an invertible function from a non-invertible function by restricting the domain.	Studied in 4th year course
F.BF.5	(+) Understand the inverse relationship between exponents and logarithms and use this relationship to solve problems involving logarithms and exponents.	Studied in 4th year course

Linear and Exponential Models*   F.LE

Construct and compare linear and exponential models and solve problems

F.LE.1	Distinguish between situations that can be modeled with linear functions and with exponential functions.	Algebra 1: 5-1, 7-8, 9-7
F.LE.1.a	Prove that linear functions grow by equal differences over equal intervals, and that exponential functions grow by equal factors over equal intervals.	Algebra 1: 9-7
F.LE.1.b	Recognize situations in which one quantity changes at a constant rate per unit interval relative to another.	Algebra 1: 5-1
F.LE.1.c	Recognize situations in which a quantity grows or decays by a constant percent rate per unit interval relative to another.	Algebra 1: 7-7
F.LE.2	Construct linear and exponential functions, including arithmetic and geometric sequences, given a graph, a description of a relationship, or two input-output pairs (include reading these from a table).	Algebra 1: 4-7, 5-3, 5-4, 5-5, 7-6, 7-8, 9-7
F.LE.3	Observe using graphs and tables that a quantity increasing exponentially eventually exceeds a quantity increasing linearly, quadratically, or (more generally) as a polynomial function.	Algebra 1: CB 9-2. 9-7
F.LE.4	For exponential models, express as a logarithm the solution to $ab^{ct} = d$ where a, c, and d are numbers and the base b is 2, 10, or e; evaluate the logarithm using technology.	Algebra 2: 7-5, 7-6

Interpret expressions for functions in terms of the situation they model

F.LE.5	Interpret the parameters in a linear or exponential function in terms of a context.	Algebra 1: 5-3, 5-4, 5-5, 5-7, 7-7

Trigonometric Functions   F.TF

Extend the domain of trigonometric functions using the unit circle

F.TF.1	Understand radian measure of an angle as the length of the arc on the unit circle subtended by the angle.	Algebra 2: 13-3
F.TF.2	Explain how the unit circle in the coordinate plane enables the extension of trigonometric functions to all real numbers, interpreted as radian measures of angles traversed counterclockwise around the unit circle.	Algebra 2: 13-4, 13-5, 13-6
F.TF.3	(+) Use special triangles to determine geometrically the values of sine, cosine, tangent for $\pi/3$, $\pi/4$ and $\pi/6$, and use the unit circle to express the values of sine, cosines, and tangent for x, $\pi + x$, and $2\pi - x$ in terms of their values for x, where x is any real number.	Studied in a 4th year course

	Functions	Where to find
F.TF.4	(+) Use the unit circle to explain symmetry (odd and even) and periodicity of trigonometric functions.	Studied in a 4th year course
Model periodic phenomena with trigonometric functions		
F.TF.5	Choose trigonometric functions to model periodic phenomena with specified amplitude, frequency, and midline.*	Algebra 2: 13-4, 13-5, 13-6, 13-7
F.TF.6	(+) Understand that restricting a trigonometric function to a domain on which it is always increasing or always decreasing allows its inverse to be constructed.	Algebra 2: 14-2
F.TF.7	(+) Use inverse functions to solve trigonometric equations that arise in modeling contexts; evaluate the solutions using technology, and interpret them in terms of the context.*	Algebra 2: 14-2
Prove and apply trigonometric identities		
F.TF.8	Prove the Pythagorean identity $\sin^2(\Theta) + \cos^2(\Theta) = 1$ and use it to calculate trigonometric ratios.	Algebra 2: 14-1
F.TF.9	(+) Prove the addition and subtraction formulas for sine, cosine, and tangent and use them to solve problems.	Algebra 2: 14-6, 14-7

Geometry		Where to find
Congruence		**G.CO**
Experiment with transformations in the plane		
G.CO.1	Know precise definitions of angle, circle, perpendicular line, parallel line, and line segment, based on the undefined notions of point, line, distance along a line, and distance around a circular arc.	Geometry: 1-2, 1-3, 1-4, 1-6, 3-1, 10-6
G.CO.2	Represent transformations in the plane using, e.g., transparencies and geometry software; describe transformations as functions that take points in the plane as inputs and give other points as outputs. Compare transformations that preserve distance and angle to those that do not (e.g., translation versus horizontal stretch).	Geometry: 9-1, 9-2, 9-3, 9-4, 9-6, CB 9-1 Algebra 2: 12-5
G.CO.3	Given a rectangle, parallelogram, trapezoid, or regular polygon, describe the rotations and reflections that carry it onto itself.	Geometry: CB 9-3
G.CO.4	Develop definitions of rotations, reflections, and translations in terms of angles, circles, perpendicular lines, parallel lines, and line segments.	Geometry: 9-1, 9-2, 9-3
G.CO.5	Given a geometric figure and a rotation, reflection, or translation, draw the transformed figure using, e.g., graph paper, tracing paper, or geometry software. Specify a sequence of transformations that will carry a given figure onto another.	Geometry: 9-1, 9-2, 9-3, 9-4, CB 9-2 Algebra 2: 12-5
Understand congruence in terms of rigid motions		
G.CO.6	Use geometric descriptions of rigid motions to transform figures and to predict the effect of a given rigid motion on a given figure; given two figures, use the definition of congruence in terms of rigid motions to decide if they are congruent.	Geometry: 9-1, 9-2, 9-3, 9-4, 9-5
G.CO.7	Use the definition of congruence in terms of rigid motions to show that two triangles are congruent if and only if corresponding pairs of sides and corresponding pairs of angles are congruent.	Geometry: 9-5
G.CO.8	Explain how the criteria for triangle congruence (ASA, SAS, and SSS) follow from the definition of congruence in terms of rigid motions.	Geometry: 9-5
Prove geometric theorems		
G.CO.9	Prove theorems about lines and angles. *Theorems include: vertical angles are congruent; when a transversal crosses parallel lines, alternate interior angles are congruent and corresponding angles are congruent; points on a perpendicular bisector of a line segment are exactly those equidistant from the segment's endpoints.*	Geometry: 2-6, 3-2, 5-2
G.CO.10	Prove theorems about triangles. *Theorems include: measures of interior angles of a triangle sum to 180°; base angles of isosceles triangles are congruent; the segment joining midpoints of two sides of a triangle is parallel to the third side and half the length; the medians of a triangle meet at a point.*	Geometry: 3-5, 4-5, 5-1, 5-4
G.CO.11	Prove theorems about parallelograms. *Theorems include: opposite sides are congruent, opposite angles are congruent, the diagonals of a parallelogram bisect each other and its converse, rectangles are parallelograms with congruent diagonals.*	Geometry: 6-2, 6-3, 6-4, 6-5

Geometry	Where to find

Make geometric constructions

| G.CO.12 | Make formal geometric constructions with a variety of tools and methods (compass and straightedge, string, reflective devices, paper folding, dynamic geometric software, etc.). *Copying a segment; copying an angle; bisecting a segment; bisecting an angle; constructing perpendicular lines, including the perpendicular bisector of a line segment; and constructing a line parallel to a given line through a point not on the line.* | Geometry: 1-6, 3-6, 4-4, 5-2, CB 3-2, CB 4-5, CB 6-9, CB 7-5 |
| G.CO.13 | Construct an equilateral triangle, a square, and a regular hexagon inscribed in a circle. | Geometry: 3-6, 4-5, 10-3 |

Similarity, Right Triangles, and Trigonometry — G.SRT

Understand similarity in terms of similarity transformations

G.SRT.1	Verify experimentally the properties of dilations given by a center and a scale factor:	Geometry: CB 9-6
G.SRT.1.a	A dilation takes a line not passing through the center of the dilation to a parallel line, and leaves a line passing through the center unchanged.	Geometry: CB 9-6
G.SRT.1.b	The dilation of a line segment is longer or shorter in the ratio given by the scale factor.	Geometry: CB 9-6
G.SRT.2	Given two figures, use the definition of similarity in terms of similarity transformations to decide if they are similar; explain using similarity transformations the meaning of similarity for triangles as the equality of all corresponding pairs of angles and the proportionality of all corresponding pairs of side.	Geometry: 9-7
G.SRT.3	Use the properties of similarity transformations to establish the AA criterion for two triangles to be similar.	Geometry: 9-7

Prove theorems involving similarity

| G.SRT.4 | Prove theorems about triangles. *Theorems include: a line parallel to one side of a triangle divides the other two proportionally and its converse; the Pythagorean Theorem proved using triangle similarity.* | Geometry: 7-5, 8-1 |
| G.SRT.5 | Use congruence and similarity criteria for triangles to solve problems and to prove relationships in geometric figures. | Geometry: 4-2, 4-3, 4-4, 4-5, 4-6, 4-7, 5-1, 5-2, 5-4, 6-1, 6-2, 6-3, 6-4, 6-5, 6-6, 7-2, 7-3, 7-4 |

Define trigonometric ratios and solve problems involving right triangles

G.SRT.6	Understand that by similarity, side ratios in right triangles are properties of the angles in the triangle, leading to definitions of trigonometric ratios for acute angles.	Algebra 1: 10-6 Geometry: CB 8-3 Algebra 2: 14-3
G.SRT.7	Explain and use the relationship between the sine and cosine of complementary angles.	Geometry: 8-3
G.SRT.8	Use trigonometric ratios and the Pythagorean Theorem to solve right triangles in applied problems.	Algebra 1: 10-1, 10-6 Geometry: 8-1, 8-2, 8-3, 8-4, CB 8-4 Algebra 2: 14-3

Apply trigonometry to general triangles

G.SRT.9	(+) Derive the formula $A = \frac{1}{2} ab \sin(C)$ for the area of a triangle by drawing an auxiliary line from a vertex perpendicular to the opposite side.	Geometry: 10-5 Algebra 2: 14-4
G.SRT.10	(+) Prove the Laws of Sines and Cosines and use them to solve problems.	Geometry: 8-5, 8-6 Algebra 2: 14-4, 14-5
G.SRT.11	(+) Understand and apply the Law of Sines and the Law of Cosines to find unknown measurements in right and non-right triangles (e.g., surveying problems, resultant forces).	Geometry: 8-5, 8-6 Algebra 2: 14-4, CB 14-4, 14-5

Circles   G.C

Understand and apply theorems about circles

G.C.1	Prove that all circles are similar.	Geometry: 10-6
G.C.2	Identify and describe relationships among inscribed angles, radii, and chords. *Include the relationship between central, inscribed, and circumscribed angles; inscribed angles on a diameter are right angles; the radius of a circle is perpendicular to the tangent where the radius intersects the circle.*	Geometry: 10-6, CB 10-6, 12-2, 12-3
G.C.3	Construct the inscribed and circumscribed circles of a triangle, and prove properties of angles for a quadrilateral inscribed in a circle.	Geometry: 5-3, 12-3
G.C.4	(+) Construct a tangent line from a point outside a given circle to the circle.	Geometry: 12-3

Find arc lengths and areas of sectors of circles

G.C.5	Derive using similarity the fact that the length of the arc intercepted by an angle is proportional to the radius, and define the radian measure of the angle as the constant of proportionality; derive the formula for the area of a sector.	Geometry: 10-6, 10-7

Expressing Geometric Properties with Equations   G.GPE

Translate between the geometric description and the equation for a conic section

G.GPE.1	Derive the equation of a circle of given center and radius using the Pythagorean Theorem; complete the square to find the center and radius of a circle given by an equation.	Geometry: 12-5 Algebra 2: 10-3, 10-6
G.GPE.2	Derive the equation of a parabola given a focus and directrix.	Geometry: CB 12-5 Algebra 2: 10-2, 10-6
G.GPE.3	(+) Derive the equations of ellipses and hyperbolas given foci and directrices.	Algebra 2: 10-4, 10-5

Use coordinates to prove simple geometric theorems algebraically

G.GPE.4	Use coordinates to prove simple geometric theorems algebraically.	Geometry: 6-9
G.GPE.5	Prove the slope criteria for parallel and perpendicular lines and use them to solve geometric problems (e.g., find the equation of a line parallel or perpendicular to a given line that passes through a given point).	Algebra 1: 5-6 Geometry: 3-8, 7-3, 7-4
G.GPE.6	Find the point on a directed line segment between two given points that partitions the segment in a given ratio.	Geometry: 1-3, 1-7
G.GPE.7	Use coordinates to compute perimeters of polygons and areas of triangles and rectangles, e.g., using the distance formula.*	Geometry: 6-7, 10-1

Geometry	Where to find
Geometric Measurement and Dimension	**G.GMD**

Explain volume formulas and use them to solve problems

G.GMD.1	Give an informal argument for the formulas for the circumference of a circle, area of a circle, volume of a cylinder, pyramid, and cone. *Use dissection arguments, Cavalieri's principle, and informal limit arguments.*	Geometry: CB 10-7, 11-4
G.GMD.2	(+) Give an informal argument using Cavalieri's principle for the formulas for the volume of a sphere and other solid figures.	Geometry: 11-4
G.GMD.3	Use volume formulas for cylinders, pyramids, cones, and spheres to solve problems*	Geometry: 11-4, 11-5, 11-6

Visualize relationships between two-dimensional and three-dimensional objects

G.GMD.4	Identify the shapes of two-dimensional cross-sections of three-dimensional objects, and identify three-dimensional objects generated by rotations of two-dimensional objects.	Geometry: 11-1, 12-6

Modeling with Geometry	**G.MG**

Apply geometric concepts in modeling situations

G.MG.1	Use geometric shapes, their measures, and their properties to describe objects (e.g., modeling a tree trunk or a human torso as a cylinder).*	Geometry: 8-3, 10-1, 10-2, 11-2, 11-3, 11-4, 11-5, 11-6, 11-7
G.MG.2	Apply concepts of density based on area and volume in modeling situations (e.g., persons per square mile, BTUs per cubic foot).*	Geometry: 11-7
G.MG.3	Apply geometric methods to solve design problems (e.g., designing an object or structure to satisfy physical constraints or minimize cost; working with typographical grid systems based on ratios).*	Geometry: 3-4

Statistics and Probability*	Where to find
Interpreting Categorical and Quantitative Data	**S.ID**

Summarize, represent, and interpret data on a single count or measurement variable

S.ID.1	Represent data with plots on the real number line (dot plots, histograms, and box plots).	Algebra 1: 12-2, 12-4
S.ID.2	Use statistics appropriate to the shape of the data distribution to compare center (median, mean) and spread (interquartile range, standard deviation) of two or more different data sets.	Algebra 1: 12-3, 12-4, CB 12-3 Algebra 2: 11-10
S.ID.3	Interpret differences in shape, center, and spread in the context of the data sets, accounting for possible effects of extreme data points (outliers).	Algebra 1: 12-3
S.ID.4	Use the mean and standard deviation of a data set to fit it to a normal distribution and to estimate population percentages. Recognize that there are data sets for which such a procedure is not appropriate. Use calculators, spreadsheets, and tables to estimate areas under the normal curve.	Algebra 2: 11-7, 11-10

Summarize, represent, and interpret data on two categorical and quantitative variables

S.ID.5	Summarize categorical data for two categories in two-way frequency tables. Interpret relative frequencies in the context of the data (including joint, marginal, and conditional relative frequencies). Recognize possible associations and trends in the data.	Algebra 1: CB 12-5
S.ID.6	Represent data on two quantitative variables on a scatter plot, and describe how the variables are related.	Algebra 1: 5-7
S.ID.6.a	Fit a function to the data; use functions fitted to data to solve problems in the context of the data. *Use given functions or choose a function suggested by the context. Emphasize linear and exponential models.*	Algebra 1: 5-7, 9-7
S.ID.6.b	Informally assess the fit of a function by plotting and analyzing residuals.	Algebra 1: CB 5-7, CB 9-7
S.ID.6.c	Fit a linear function for a scatter plot that suggests a linear association.	Algebra 1: 5-7

Interpret linear models

S.ID.7	Interpret the slope (rate of change) and the intercept (constant term) of a linear model in the context of the data.	Algebra 1: 5-7
S.ID.8	Compute (using technology) and interpret the correlation coefficient of a linear fit.	Algebra 1: 5-7
S.ID.9	Distinguish between correlation and causation.	Algebra 1: 5-7
Making Inferences and Justifying Conclusions		**S.IC**

Understand and evaluate random processes underlying statistical experiments

S.IC.1	Understand statistics as a process for making inferences to be made about population parameters based on a random sample from that population.	Algebra 2: 11-8
S.IC.2	Decide if a specified model is consistent with results from a given data-generating process, e.g., using simulation.	Algebra 2: CB 11-3

Make inferences and justify conclusions from sample surveys, experiments, and observational studies

S.IC.3	Recognize the purposes of and differences among sample surveys, experiments, and observational studies; explain how randomization relates to each.	Algebra 1: 12-5, CB 12-5 Algebra 2: 11-8
S.IC.4	Use data from a sample survey to estimate a population mean or proportion; develop a margin of error through the use of simulation models for random sampling.	Algebra 2: 11-8, CB 11-10a

		Statistics and Probability*	**Where to find**
S.IC.5		Use data from a randomized experiment to compare two treatments; use simulations to decide if differences between parameters are significant.	Algebra 1: 12-7 Algebra 2: CB 11-10b
S.IC.6		Evaluate reports based on data.	Algebra 2: 11-6, 11-7, 11-8

Conditional Probability and the Rules of Probability — S.CP

Understand independence and conditional probability and use them to interpret data

S.CP.1		Describe events as subsets of a sample space (the set of outcomes) using characteristics (or categories) of the outcomes, or as unions, intersections, or complements of other events ("or," "and," "not").	Algebra 1: 12-7 Geometry: 13-1
S.CP.2		Understand that two events A and B are independent if the probability of A and B occurring together is the product of their probabilities, and use this characterization to determine if they are independent.	Algebra 1: CB 12-9 Geometry: 13-6 Algebra 2: 11-3
S.CP.3		Understand the conditional probability of A given B as $P(A \text{ and } B)/P(B)$, and interpret independence of A and B as saying that the conditional probability of A given B is the same as the probability of A, and the conditional probability of B given A is the same as the probability of B.	Algebra 1: CB 12-9 Geometry: 13-6 Algebra 2: 11-4
S.CP.4		Construct and interpret two-way frequency tables of data when two categories are associated with each object being classified. Use the two-way table as a sample space to decide if events are independent and to approximate conditional probabilities.	Algebra 1: 12-7 Geometry: 13-1, 13-2, 13-5 Algebra 2: 11-4
S.CP.5		Recognize and explain the concepts of conditional probability and independence in everyday language and everyday situations.	Algebra 1: CB 12-9 Geometry: 13-2, 13-6 Algebra 2: 11-3, 11-4

Use the rules of probability to compute probabilities of compound events in a uniform probability model

S.CP.6		Find the conditional probability of A given B as the fraction of B's outcomes that also belong to A, and interpret the answer in terms of the model.	Geometry: 13-6 Algebra 2: 11-4
S.CP.7		Apply the Addition Rule, $P(A \text{ or } B) = P(A) + P(B) - P(A \text{ and } B)$, and interpret the answer in terms of the model.	Algebra 1: 12-8 Geometry: 13-4 Algebra 2: 11-3
S.CP.8		(+) Apply the general Multiplication Rule in a uniform probability model, $P(A \text{ and } B) = P(A)P(B|A) = P(B)P(A|B)$, and interpret the answer in terms of the model.	Algebra 1: 12-8 Geometry: 13-4 Algebra 2: 11-4
S.CP.9		(+) Use permutations and combinations to compute probabilities of compound events and solve problems.	Geometry: 13-4 Algebra 2: 11-1

Using Probability to Make Decisions — S.MD

Calculate expected values and use them to solve problems

S.MD.1		(+) Define a random variable for a quantity of interest by assigning a numerical value to each event in a sample space; graph the corresponding probability distribution using the same graphical displays as for data distributions.	Studied in a 4th year course
S.MD.2		(+) Calculate the expected value of a random variable; interpret it as the mean of the probability distribution.	Studied in a 4th year course

Statistics and Probability*		Where to find
S.MD.3	(+) Develop a probability distribution for a random variable defined for a sample space in which theoretical probabilities can be calculated; find the expected value.	Studied in a 4th year course
S.MD.4	(+) Develop a probability distribution for a random variable defined for a sample space in which probabilities are assigned empirically; find the expected value.	Studied in a 4th year course
Use probability to evaluate outcomes of decisions		
S.MD.5	(+) Weigh the possible outcomes of a decision by assigning probabilities to payoff values and finding expected values.	Studied in a 4th year course
S.MD.5.a	(+) Find the expected payoff for a game of chance.	Studied in a 4th year course
S.MD.5.b	(+) Evaluate and compare strategies on the basis of expected values.	Studied in a 4th year course
S.MD.6	(+) Use probabilities to make fair decisions (e.g., drawing by lots, using a random number generator).	Geometry: 13-7, CB 13-7 Algebra 2: 11-5
S.MD.7	(+) Analyze decisions and strategies using probability concepts (e.g., product testing, medical testing, pulling a hockey goalie at the end of a game).	Geometry: 13-7, CB 13-7 Algebra 2: 11-5